AF668398

A Poem

Joseph Hart

Copyright© 2023 Joseph Hart
ISBN: 978-81-19228-05-8

First Edition: 2023
Rs. 200/-

Cyberwit.net
HIG 45 Kaushambi Kunj, Kalindipuram
Allahabad - 211011 (U.P.) India
http://www.cyberwit.net
Tel: +(91) 9415091004
E-mail: info@cyberwit.net

No part of this book may be reproduced or transmitted in any form or by any means, electronic, mechanical, photocopying, or otherwise, without the express written consent of Joseph Hart.

The solipsistic nothingness of dreams
Seems substantial when I am asleep.
I wish that I could sleep while I'm awake
Thus to know the meaning of my dreams.
Are dreams sincere? As what I do or say?
Remember, think or feel? - How often I
Remember what did not occur at all!
Is this some insincerity in me?
Is sleep sincere? - The sweetest truth of all!
The kindest honesty that ever was!
And poesy can make of sleep a thing,
A deep enchantment sensually felt.
But when I sleep, I am myself alone;
And then when I engage in poesy
I conjure up a ready page,
A page of ready sleep,
And summon up a seeming page,
A page of seeming sleep
And call the things I think therein a dream.
A soothing song can put my soul to sleep
Where it awakens in a gentle dream.
I think I feel what only is a dream:
A dream of sleep that's manifold with dreams.
And when I sleep, I can become the ocean,
In spirit if not fact become the sea.
And this image seems more factual than souls.
I muse in empty hours over which
Is the better understanding of the two:
When I sleep or when I am awake?
My waking doesn't understand a thing.

My sleeping understands my wakefulness
And also understands another thing
And changes understanding into dreams.
But poesy can put the heart to sleep
And thereby let it dream forevermore
The warmest things that ever have been thought.
So therefore let me, drunk with poesy,
Maunder through a colloquy of dreams,
A dialectic of soliloquy.
Or let me in a litany of senses
Summon up ideas that are warm
Or soft as sleep, or softer than a touch is.
And if I hear the ocean in a poem
Or sense a ghost (the shadow of a life)
It will endear the poem more to me
Than any other soothing quality.
When sudden from heaven like a gentle rain,
Or slowly, like a weary traveler
Sleep's shadow comes to cover over me.
Bemused and thoughtless, vacant and self-conscious,
I lie upon the pillows of my arms
And dream of things. And such is poesy.
When sleep appears, upsurging and anon
And fills my body, head to foot to hand,
I waft as does a ghost upon the wind,
I float as does a bird upon the air
And touch the surface of my mental skin,
But touch it lightly, once and then again;
And then at last into the depth of me,
Into my stomach I begin to sleep
With every area of body there,

Both felt and feeling. Sleep becomes the air.
Securely as a hypnotizing hand,
Old sleep succumbs to heavy-lidded slumber,
And dreams that follow in the wake of sleep
Encourage it by closing waking's door.
When I undertake an understanding sleep
It makes an exorcism of my soul
And brings fey ghosts and shadows from my past
All once again into the open air
But differently, not as once they were
When they occurred, but with a difference:
A fantasy derived from memory.
I walk into the tired house of sleep,
Descend the stairs, and dream until I wake.
But sleep's an exorcist, make no mistake;
It summons ghosts forgotten or unthought,
And in the darkness of my sleep
Reveals them in the light of dreams.
The characters from out my past
Enact another play,
A deep but other story
Then when I knew them once
When I'm asleep and dreaming.
Asleep I am at once!
Poesy and oceans, ghosts and sleep
And music are the essence of my life,
Not held aloft upon my finger-tips
But savored to the fullest of my depth.
And when it's night and all the glass is dark,
Sleep's the gentlest of experience.
Sleep knows the things I know when I'm awake;

But waking does not understand the dream.
Enchanting and enchanted sleep
Comes slowly and anon;
I'm not aware when I have gone asleep.
The breath of sleep inspires sudden dreams,
A breathing sleep much free-er than my life;
And if I were a convict in a cell,
I'd still have sleep wherewith to set me free.
Each morning I remember once again
That I've yielded to the sweet cessation, sleep;
When conscious only of the things I dream
I've felt the perfect solitude of sleep.
Gentle sleep, sincerely gentle sleep
Abrogates my senses,
And I see nothing but the heart of me.
A sleep supplants external consciousness
With slumber and with consciousness of dreams.
Old sleep's a ghost; the ocean is its home.
And all throughout the echoes of a dream
I hear the sullen thud of ocean waves.
The surf breaks on the beach of wakefulness;
And sleep's the surf. It carries me to sea.
And out at sea, I sail into the storms,
The maelstroms and storms of gentle dreams.
Much older than the breath of dinosaurs,
Old sleep is old. As I am used to it,
So each new sleep seems older than the last.
As sleep, so love. Each time new love is new.
But I've become accustomed to the thing.
And each new lover feels familiar.
Each time I sleep, it feels the same to me.

Yet I rejoice! For every sleep is new.
I crave old sleep, forever young and new,
Both at once: forever old and new.
And when I wish to dream, I need but think
That I'm asleep: for sleep, already there.
Appoint me now to sleep, my perfect dream!
Awaken me to dreams, my gentle sleep.
The kiss of sleep is like a mother's hand
Upon my forehead while I fall asleep.
I rest my tired body on the bed
And revel in sensations of new sleep.
Come quickly, magic sleep, and bring to me
The deep enchantment of another dream!
Magic sleep and sleepy magic give to me
The fascination of a vivid dream
That deep exegesis will counteract,
Dissolve into the currency of day,
Quotidian, the banal commonplace
Of living. Ah, but when I sleep again!
Another dream in shrouded mystery,
Colorful and piquant and profound,
Will come to take its place; and I will dream.
When sleep is in me, on the underside
Of my skin, I feel it everywhere.
When sleep is on me, I am sound asleep.
With music that's appropriate for sleep
And sleep that is appropriate for dreams.
I lie abed and dream myself to sleep.
My new loves seems familiar to me;
First loves are best. And so it is with sleep:
How did I feel the first time that I slept?

But what is time to sleep? Or sleep to time?
Dreams have no time except their own emotion.
If heaven is a great eternity
Of mindless pleasure, what is wrong with sex?
Or love? Or sleep? Or anything that pleases?
Pleasure is the solitary test.
If gods condemn this ecstasy,
Then I prefer no gods.
And sleep, it is a gentle ecstasy.
And pleasure is the true and only proof.
When I was psychotic, sleep came deeply
To quell the clamor of the noisome day.
I don't remember any dreams I had;
I did my dreaming when I was awake.
The essence of those dreams was rich with color,
Interest and coruscating thought.
Out of the province of insensate sleep,
Those dreams abounded in the wakeful day
Surrounded, though, by intermittent sleeps.
It was a strange concatenation of events,
These waking dreams and deeply dreamless sleeps
Alternating. When I slept it was
The dreamless depth of the unghosted dead.
But now I sleep; and when I sleep I say
Lightly to touch the surface of a dream,
Lightly to touch the surface of the skin
To summon feeling with the merest touch
Like breathing on a winter windowpane.
But don't neglect to sound the fullest depth
And thoroughly to say the thing completely.
Afraid of making other people angry?

I am so much it dominates my life,
Controls whatever thoughts that I may think
And absolutely what I do and say.
But as I fall asleep, I have no fears
But only do succumb to subtlety,
Illusion, myth and tenderest sensation.
Sleep is the gentle harvester of gold!
It makes the coward brave and unafraid
And gives him to a sweet equality.
It offers its surcease to the infirm,
And with its pleasant touch, it seems to heal.
There is no death in sleep, but only dreams.
Sleep's the tender counterpart of love.
I am afraid of making people angry.
It makes of me a liar and a sneak.
But sleep's restorative ineffable
Both soft and safe for dreaming softer dreams
Gives me a place among a world of peers,
Dissolves and obfuscates my sordid fears.
Death is not sleep, nor sleep the counterfeit
Of death; they are not similar at all.
In one, romance is living in the brain
As breath escapes the wholesome, parted lips.
In the other there is nothing but decay,
Unless a ghost flees fitful from the fall
And goes at large amid a greater sleep.
But, ah! The tender refutation of a dream
Inhabits houses full of sentiments:
The eyes and noses and senses of the mind!
And touch, sweet touch, the origin of all,
All waking and all sleep and all in all!

Touch has a memory, but doesn't know
What I will dream until the dream is there.
When my love sleeps, I cannot see his dreams
Nor hear the conversations in his brain,
But only see the look upon his face.
Benign, it is the countenance of sleep.
My love is never farther off from me
Than when he sleeps; then he is far away.
I've only to arouse him to be near.
Heard melodies are sweet; but those unheard
Are sweeter. Therefore let dear sleep dream on.
I think I am as phony as a dream
That is not either factual or true,
With meaning esoteric and arcane.
I think I am as phony as a dream,
And all my soul a long recondite sleep.
Grey and white, the seagull sits with folded wings
Upon the pier post sunk into the sea.
A piece of rope is wrapped around the post.
The surge of this dynamic, dismal sea
Reminds me of the time I was asleep.
And I conceive an image of deep sleep.
Keats' picture hanging warm upon my wall
Bemused and pensive gazes into space.
In looking at it, I feel much of sleep
That overcomes me like a pleasant dream.
Eternal and immortal present sleep!
Past sleeps and present sleep and sleeps to come!
Sleep is a metaphor for sleep itself.
I live in the imaginings of sleep,
A deep-imagined, unimagined sleep.

I live in an imaginary sleep
That laps across my senses and my mind
As sea waves in a sweet concatenation
Spread across the everlasting shore
Or fill a grotto once and once again
And leave it empty in the interims,
Fill with hollow echoes from the water.
This would be all a friendly place to sleep
Were I a ghost without a house to haunt.
Deep sleep comes like an ancient summer calm
And soothes my soul to rest and peaceful dreams.
But sleep is like a ghost
Intangible and free
That settles on me with its nothingness
Of feeling. I can see the Parthenon
In gentle balance that resembles sleep.
How many lovely sayings can I make
About the deep enchantment of soft sleep?
I simply wish to say some pretty things.
All my truths are solitary ones.
I feel a sense of sleep while looking at
Junkets' picture hanging on the wall,
A downy sleep, pervasive, soft and sensive.
Succumbing to the wholesome spell of sleep,
A gentle trance that houses who I am,
I conjure up the magic of dead sleep
As if my body had been hypnotized
With sleep the hypnotist, and dreams the hand
That makes the passes mesmerizing me.
Soft sleep comes soft as some unsummoned calm
And conjures images inside of me.

Such images themselves are half the cause
Of sleep itself that soothes my body's form.
There is an ocean regular as breath
On the desolate and solitary shore.
There's verse in sleep, in sleep a poesy,
A deep, enchanting, soft, enchanted sleep.
There's poesy in sleep, of sleep, asleep
That allows the dreams of dreamers isolate.
Though I begin self-conscious of my sleep
I very soon drift into fantasy
Where I both am myself and see myself
In a paradox of dual consciousness.
I feel a docile sleep come over me
While I am lying all alone in bed;
And I become more passive when I'm sleeping
And yielding to a rich and fragrant dream.
The sandy Sphinx is made of sleepy rock
And gazes out with majesty
Across the desert shore,
Strange withal, and nonetheless asleep.
The Sphinx is dead and preternatural;
It looks into the distance half-asleep.
The Parthenon is neither dead nor strange,
But lives in sleep that time has yet to ruin.
I think I am asleep, and so I am
In that dark, wall-less chamber of my heart
Where fantasies can flourish while I sleep
And make a rendez-vous of rhapsody.
In warm surrender, sleep can be my god,
A god that I can touch and think and feel.
This formless sleep must be my deity.

Sleep has no form except my body's shape.
Amorphous spectre, occupy my soul
And let your outline be my body's own.
Sleep is at the very core of poesy.
All pleasures merge and mingle into sleep.
All other pleasures are but one: asleep.
When drowsiness can occupy my skull
And wake a yawning appetite for sleep,
I nestle nurtured into my own soul
And sleep and dream till morning wakens me.
A house of clouds, a room of pleasant sleep!
Or to float alone upon the soul of night
Dreaming sleepily and unaware!
If I am haunted by the ghost of sleep,
Then it's as if my body were a house,
And sleep's the shade that occupies it there,
Maundering down corridors and halls,
Passing among chambers one by one.
And at the casements of my lidded eyes,
Old sleep looks out: a solitary ghost.
(Junkets was a genius without talent;
I carry on where Junkets just began
And consummate my efforts with a sleep.)
Good sleep is just a whisper in the night,
Two soft lips pressing close upon my ear
And telling me, "Good sleep until tomorrow."
Good sleep, heart-nourished sleep, be fond of me!
Be like a mother to my wanting soul,
Half drowsy from the fragrant trance of poppies,
And lower me into your timeless grave!
The fragrance of such poppies makes a trance

Whose scent arouses comfortable sleep
To overtake and disencumber me
Until I'm like a cobweb in a breeze,
A filament that wafts
Among the currents of the air,
Settling often here, as often there.
Oh, for a field of poppies
Upon a summer day
Whose scent's entrancing fragrance makes me sleep
There in that field of poppies
Upon that summer day!
To make of dreams a soothing roundelay!
If in my body's sleep or in myself
I find a subject fit for poesy,
I'll make a soothing verse of who I am,
As if my body's very meat and bone
Were suitable as subjects for a song.
Any subject's suitable. The thing
Is poesy: the poem is the thing
That matters. Ah, to make a gentle dream
Of healthy sleep to succor the unloved,
Unloving or unwanting any love!
Fair sleep's a sage, affectionate and soft
That knows whereof I dream, which I do not.
Engulfed in sound as if in sleep,
This music is a rhapsody.
Surrounded, drowned in wholesome sound,
This music is asleep.
And forward-looking, atavistic dreams,
As substantial as an insubstantial yawn,
Come softly from the nothingness of me,

As well as from the nothingness of sleep,
And make a slight phantasm of my sleep.
These sleep-inducing soporific dreams
Are less profound than sleep, than sleep itself.
If I could live forever in some dreams
(Like poesy), the nothingness of dreams
Surrounded by the nothingness of sleep,
I'd be forever happier than now.
These gentle dreams, soft, incorporeal,
All seem substantial as my very hand,
And yet they are as vacant as the air,
Sweet cloudy myths that I have not the hands
To grasp and hold and keep forevermore,
But lose as time progresses after sleep.
Forgetfulness succeeds awakening.
Yet for some hours after I have slept,
I carry like a taste upon my tongue
The sweet aroma of this after-sleep
And the memory of dreams I dreamt therein.
At last they're like an empty spider's web,
All blown to tatters by the passing breezes,
Torn and broken and dispersed and gone
Till just a random filament remains.
So what I dreamed at last will disappear
Into forgetfulness and leave behind
Slight memories, some tokens of the dream,
Perhaps a few remembrances evoked
By somethings that occur throughout the day.
But most of what I dreamt will disappear,
Forever vanish in eternal night.
But sleep will come again and with it bring

New dreams for old to occupy my mind.
Concatenate, a gentle chain of dreams
With each one unrelated to the others
Surfeits my brain while I am sound asleep.
How soft the sounds that summon sleep,
A single sense invoking
That covers me as if I were
Immersed in tender water.
And everywhere I'm touched by sleep,
A gentle hand caressing.
And all the senses that I have
Feel sleep in all its tenses,
Future, past and present sleep.
And dreaming recommences.
Old sleep is like the ocean or a poem;
My single heart can feel the darkness there
As it succumbs to sleep's intoxication.
And sleep is like a poem; or the sea
Whose lifting waves come closer to the shore,
Engulf it once, as in a deep pulsation
Or ardent heartbeat, then withdraw to sea.
When I am drunk, profoundly drunk with sleep,
I see the images inside my head
And watch the stories that they claim to tell.
Distinctly I hear voices in my mind
In conversation's corresponding dreams.
Awash with sleep, I plunge into the grave
Of sleep, sink deeper and awaken on
The other side of sleep, into a dream.
I yawn and feel my body in my mind,
A single eye that wishes for new sleep.

I ope the magic casement of my soul
And feel aware as deep sleep rushes in
To fill my body with its honesty.
I think there is sincerity in sleep.
And conscious, then, of consciousness I dream.
Another night, another consciousness
Of sleep, another consciousness of dreams
Will take me still more fully into what
Is me, is deep, is paradisiacal.
A sleepy heart replete with many dreams
Can fall asleep and see them all come true.
A sleepy night, dream-laden, can befall
A person who is not asleep at all.
Exhausted sleep can summon happiness
To eyes that shut at first in misery,
And out of an exhaustive sense of dreams,
Can make a spell for disenchanted eyes.
Is there some sensuality in sleep
Besides the sexuality of dreams?
Is there a temple of forgetfulness
Beside which sleep, the naked river, runs?
The hands of slumber hypnotize my heart
And give the soft enchantment of a dream
To eyes that wake, but only so in sleep.
The shades of darkness tenderly describe
A warm circumference around my form
In which my heart is ready for a dream,
In whose circle I am apt to undertake
The ready, warm commencement of a dream.
Peradventure, the sacrament of sleep
Is holy in its sacred ecstasy.

And sexuality is sacred too,
And holy in its randy rhapsody.
All sex is good; but sleep is better still
And starts with the beginning of a dream.
But which comes first: the dreamer or his sleep?
Beginning with a dream, I end up sleeping.
I start with sleep, and soon I'm in a dream.
I can relax until sleep overcomes me,
Overtakes my senses and I sleep.
Soon after (qui sait quand?) I start to dream.
And I can begin by thinking of a dream
I've had before, and find that I'm asleep.
To make a pretty thing of pretty sleep
Is all this poesy aspires to do.
In all the poems that I ever wrote
I only wished to make a happy thing,
Even when I wrote about myself.
But then I wished to re-experience,
Make manifest, objectify
A person or a moment in my life.
What do I write? I write what pleases me.
What do I write? I write what I enjoy.
And Proust himself declared that this is all
A writer who's mature will write about -
Not that he should, but only that he will.
I only wished to make a novelty
And to be considered good at what I do.
Now let sleep come as some unsummoned calm
To soothe away the tensions and regrets
And give my heart the commonplace of love.
Let music soft dissolve me into sleep,

And in this dissolution, let me dream
A fantasy, an alchemy of love.
And often in the afterward of sleep
I find myself remembering a dream.
It brings with it remembrances of sleep
And sleep's aroma and its feel in me.
As often in sleep's deep forgetfulness
As in the full forgetfulness of dreams
I find myself remembering a way
I'd never thought of when I was awake.
But the tender dissipation
Of this notion in the dawn
Makes me wonder who I am asleep.
The thunder of the ocean on the shore
Is all-engulfing as a gentle sleep;
But in the ocean I can see no dreams
Unless I am remembering the sea.
The ocean is a harbinger of sleep,
And sleep is the soft bringer of soft dreams.
Now leave me to a manifold of sleeps,
And with each sleep, a manifold of dreams.
I'll crawl into the darkling cave of sleep
And therein find the colored toy of dreams.
How serious the sleeper is,
The dreamer is at play!
Where is the origin of what I dream?
What is the source of these enchanted scenes?
What do these surrealistic stories mean
That come unquenched from somewhere in my soul?
Have they a meaning that I can define
That mystify my sleep-untroubled mind?

Delicious sleep has got no enemies,
But is a tender presence to all things.
Sleep is not warm, but soft and sensuous.
Sleep is the equalizer of all life
In the family of mortal consciousness.
Come what matters, come what seems;
Present sleep has present dreams.
Sequestered in a region of deep sleep,
I watch the softest dreams come into me,
Participate in these strange phantoms' play
And feel the wealth and rhapsody of dreaming.
This fragrant sleep has only one emotion,
And dreams are like an ecstasy of sense.
Beneath the gentle wing of the warm night
I summon up the shadow of soft sleep.
In sleep's shadow is my heart aware
Of the deep substantial nothingness of dreams
With details rich my sleeping eyes can see,
Seeming more so than when I'm awake.
I see more details in a sleeping dream
Than ever did I when I was awake
See in the waking world surrounding me.
My dreams are like the shadows of my sleep;
My sleep is like the shadow of a dream.
Good sleep is proof against the coming night
When all have gone to darkness (lost in dreams).
And I become a dream each time I sleep
As surely as I can become the sea
By sitting on a rock and watching it.
But seldom do I dream about the sea,
As seldom do I dream about a ghost

Or anything that matters most to me.
I rarely dream of the familiar,
But conjure up the preternatural.
My dreams combine the things that I can touch
Into a story I have never seen.
The deep invention of a warmer dream!
Allow me in the empty cave of sleep
To summon up some shadows on the walls
All full of many colors, many sounds,
And therein let these dreams be all of me:
As I become them, they are all of me.
At night as I lie snuggled in my bed,
There is no more to me than what I dream.
I am a dream in insulating sleep.
Those disparate elements that make a dream
All come together in a sweet alliance,
A strange agreement that makes sense to sleep.
Dreams are a sleepy ecstasy of senses
Combining the familiar and strange
Into a prototypical delight.
Come rock me gently in the arms of sleep
As if my heart were cradled by the sea,
Rocked gently by the shoulder-lapping waves.
As if I were a boat upon the water
Riding peacefully the ocean's heaves,
Come sing to me a song of drowsiness
And lull me into rest and sleepy dreams.
Is the sea as deep as sleep?
Are dreams familiar and strange
As was the world when I perceived it first?
Are dreams the poesy of sleep?

Is poesy a dream
Ensconced in sleep as if remembering?
And the inconclusive ending of a dream
Puts me in mind of Mozart's own concertos.
I am alone within the image, sleep;
And afterward come gravid dreams
That give me company.
Soft music gently ushers me to sleep
Where dreams come out as phantoms do at night
And show their secrets to my sleeping heart
That participates in what they do and say
But will not understand them when I wake.
How can my heart take part in what I dream
But fail to understand it when I wake?
Together and alone, my heart and I
Can occupy a dream-enchanted sleep.
Together and alone, my heart and I
Find refuge in a sleep-enchanted dream.
Thalassic sleep that eddies in my soul
And draws me to the center of the storm
Where all is peaceful, restful and serene,
Soothes my body with soft-handed slumber
And makes me wake into an ecstasy,
A rhapsody of dreams I'll comprehend
For the moment, until I awake.
Throughout the night I hear the ocean roar.
I'm sheltered in the shadow of the sea.
It thunders on time's dark, eternal shore
While I rest fondly in the arms of sleep
And dream of things I quasi-recognize.
I lie in the embrace of subtle sleep.

When I fall under Junkets' magic spell,
Or else the spell of any poesy,
I feel asleep although I am awake;
Which makes me think all pleasure is like sleep.
Sleep's gentle kiss upon my countenance
Assures me through the long, eternal night
That there's a presence underneath my covers
Involved in the enchantment of a dream,
The personal enchantment of a dream.
Sleep's suction on my psyche
Keeps me buried under sleep,
Although I wake to noises in the hall.
When I was young, I wandered everywhere
And never found a place to settle in.
And sleeping was my only constancy,
My world's one single regularity;
And yet it merged into my maundering
As if my heart were all the time asleep
And never woke. An old, enchanted thing!
My dreams seem sensible while I'm asleep
And for an hour after I awake.
But later on, they seem detached, bizarre,
But nonetheless a pleasure to recall.
Remembered dreams put me to sleep again.
Sleepy magic, magic sleep can make
My dreams come true, but only while I sleep.
To sleep upon a raft and slowly drift,
And wake two hours later out at sea
Is both my horror and my fantasy!
This was a dream I had the other night.
I don't know what I'll dream until I dream it.

It comes as something foreign to my eyes.
And yet it is my very heart's creation.
Why don't I know what I am going to dream?
I ought to know what I am going to dream.
But to enjoy a dream completely
Is the essence of the night,
Surrounded by a disincarnate sleep,
Embedded in a disenchanted sleep.
To enjoy a dream completely
On the surface of soft sleep,
To wake, and then to catch the dream again
Renewing an acquaintance with new sleep
Is warmly tender ecstasy, is whole!
I lately slept uncomfortable asleep.
My dreams were empty, vacant and remote
And kept me half-awake throughout the night,
Though now I don't recall a single one.
The Christian gods are evil;
The Christians merely bad.
But sleep can seal them up as in a tomb,
Shut their eyes and still their execrations,
And for an hour, there is peacefulness.
Of all nice things, deep sleep must be the nicest!
And to be nice to all the little live things
And Freedom are my sole morality.
(Not to be nice may possibly be bad;
Not to be Free is impermissible.)
But sex (pre-, post- and extra-marital)
And promiscuity were never bad.
And censorship's as wicked as the grave!
And homosexuality is good.

Pornography is just a harmless pleasure.
And prostitution never hurt a thing.
Nor do I deal in sordid or debased
Matters in considering these things;
They're all a part of earth and life and love.
And sleep itself's a lonely kind of love;
But it dissolves away all earthly woes
And gives me the enchantment of a dream.
Soft music hypnotizes me to sleep,
To mesmerize me out of consciousness
And into consciousness of my sole soul
Wherein I'll see the shadow of a dream,
Wherein I'll be the shadow of a dream.
Where oceans rise around my every side
And thunderous fog moves across the shore
I'll savor the enigma of a dream
And not until I wake will I endeavor
To understand the riddles of my sleep.
I'll wake asleep into a wealth of dreams,
Enveloped in the feeling of deep sleep.
I'll sail upon the shallow tide of dreams,
Or out upon the deep, deep sea of sleep.
I'll feel the ocean while I sleep;
The sea is deep within me.
And all that matters I recall
In slumber without music.
I don't care whether there are gods or not.
I do care whether there's an afterlife.
Ah, to be a ghost, invisible and free
And waft like dreams down darkling corridors
Alive, alone in an enchanted sleep!

Let death be sleep, but only if I dream!
I think I'd rather dream than be awake.
The silliest things seem sensible
At night while I am dreaming.
I think I am psychotic while I sleep.
And sleep itself can make a thing
Seem sensible and real.
What is this magical and wondrous sleep,
As sweet as music in a lover's arms?
Last night I heard some music while I slept.
Like a phantom passing through hard walls,
This music passed through my transparent sleep
And became a central figure in my dream.
I found it in the dream that I was dreaming,
This music that was playing while I slept.
I found it in the sense that I was dreaming,
This music that occurred outside of me.
Why do I often feel deep recognition
For something that I see inside a dream,
A something I have never seen before,
Whether sleeping or awake have never seen?
How can I recognize while I am dreaming
Something I have never seen before?
But sleep is whole, as sails upon a ship
All full of wind that blows them cross the sea.
I love the sweet sincerity of sleep
That lets the face relax into repose,
Free as an Atheist's heart. God hates the truth!
The subtlest of deaths: to die asleep,
And see no more the evening or the dawn,
But there to lapse beneath a shadow's dream.

Dreams cast shadows far beyond the night.
There's nothing superficial in a dream,
Though it may touch the surface of the mind,
It has its roots deep in the dreamer's heart.
Were I to sleep and never wake again,
Then all my dreams would be reality;
And among the phantoms fey I'd be a ghost
That goes from dream to dream inside my mind
In the concatenatious evolution of my dreams.
I dreamt I walked into a pole
And woke up with a jump!
So what on earth can such a symbol mean?
Colliding with the pole so startled me
It woke me with a jerk. And yet I must
Have known the pole was there: I made the dream.
Yet waking from collision with the pole
Does seem a natural consequence of things.
And people are like beasties in a cage,
(A cage of windows, but with no way out);
A few of many think about the cage,
The others are content with happiness
Until the hand of death has plucked them out
And set them on the other side of sleep.
And me, I am content with poesy:
It is the only air that I can breathe.
As blocks of ice stay big into the morning
But melt and disappear throughout the day,
So do I recollect my dreams at dawn,
All lucid, rich and full of images
That melt and disappear as time goes by,
Until scant and pallid images remain,

Like little chunks of ice left on the lawn,
Remnants of the blasting heat of noon.
How many lovely sayings can I say
About my oldest, deepest, dearest friend:
Good sleep and pleasant dreams that follow after?
I think of the phenomenon of sleep
And slowly feel my heart becoming drowsy.
And the warm reiteration of a dream
(Remembering a dream I had before)
Encourages a wave of sleep to pass
(Alike the hand of any hypnotist)
Across my mind and body in the night.
And each of us has loved and lost
And been the loved one lost;
So I think there are no secrets anymore.
But sleep is more a solace than a bond.
With memory too bitter to perceive
That turns the flames of presence undergone,
It has to take some time until the past
Is suitable a distance far away
To sentimentalize
The ruins and remains
And give them life, that have life of their own.
To see again the people of my past!
To introduce a spectre, kiss a ghost!
To savor a remark or comment made
And relish in the pleasure of the feel
Of this remark in its remembering!
To feel as if I'd found the lock
To which it is the key!
Limp-wristed youth may stand with wind-mussed hair

And smile as if it were the morning sun;
And all is fluid, natural and warm.
I never was so natural as this;
I always was an awkward little man;
But nonetheless I can appreciate
That which I can't conceive, imagine, do.
Fair sleep removes the swaddling from my soul
And leaves me free to do howe'er I please.
Everyone is beautiful asleep,
If only to himself, alone, asleep.
Old sleep makes paradise of commonplace.
In drunken sleep with dreams I don't recall
I rest in deathly slumber until dawn.
Unsummoned comes inebriated sleep
Up from my body's core into my skin
Until both depth and surface are the same:
All haunted by a deep and shallow sleep.
Truth is no other than reality,
Surrounded by its little hills of sleep.
There is no bigger, greater truth than this.
And if there were, it only would be real:
A phenomenon to be adjusted to
Until it has become a commonplace.
To sleep, to sleep, to sleep and then to dream
What the waking world will never understand!
To sleep, to sleep, to sleep, to sleep, to dream
And then to wake and feel it fade away!
To dream I do a thing, but not to do it -
A repetitious dream that keeps my slumber
Until I wake and do the thing I dream
Is magical enchantment made of sleep.

But often comes a beneficial dream
That I remember all throughout the day
And wish that it would come again,
Although it never does;
And it is lost, forever lost and gone.
And I shall never understand
And never feel again
The magic of this beneficial dream.
I do remember some of what I dreamed,
But not so fully as I dreamed it then.
I do remember how this dream once felt,
But not so deep as when I dreamed it then.
Soft sleep, the gentle bringer of fey dreams
Renders brains unbigoted and warm,
Free and open as of any child.
Soft sleep is the soft bringer of soft dreams.
Last night I had a dream within a dream.
I dreamed that I was sound asleep and dreaming,
And dreamt a dream inside the dream I dreamt.
Most tenderly to tumble into sleep,
Drift drowsily and dreamily to sleep
Can almost make the day a thing to love.
Awash with sudden memories
(Especially of nights before)
Can subtle me to sleep,
As if into a fog of gentle warmth
I were led. I eat my dreams,
Digest them into spectral sleep,
And suddenly I'm in the shadow's arms!
Sleep as a shadow hovers over me,
And under me and in me and around

Until the room and all its furniture
Have faded into everlasting darkness
And there is only left a bed of sleep.
While I'm tucked away in bed,
Things can happen in my dreams
That happen nowhere else.
Because a thing is false, shall I infer
That its antithesis is therefore true?
I think not; but sleep resolves all doubt.

How many, many sayings can I say
About a pretty sleep, that conjurer?
Fair sleep's the conjurer of pretty things.
Deep sleep is the magician that reveals
All mystery, all magic and all love;
Without it they would none of them exist.
My daydreams sparkle like the night,
But then I do not dwell in them;
I wait for darkness to come out
To inhabit there uninterrupted dreams.

unfinished
January - March, 1987

www.ingramcontent.com/pod-product-compliance
Lightning Source LLC
Chambersburg PA
CBHW022204160726
48282CB00024B/323
* 9 7 8 8 1 1 9 2 2 8 0 5 8 *